"Learning to regulate the chatter"

This book contains the framework of the five (5) mental skills and a personal roadmap for development. Your new goals will include self-awareness and self-regulation and the objective is to regulate disruptive thoughts and distracting emotions. This is my best effort to help you bridge the gap between who you are and your true potential. These ideas are based on the newly revealed truths found in the field of Neuroscience and the learned behaviors supported in the study of Emotional Intelligence.

Parrish Owen Taylor

To my children:

Learning, living and applying these ideas in my own life I have worked hard to lead you by example. The ideas, the words in this book are my best effort to simplify this complicated study of "self". Based on scripture and supported by new science, what we are now learning is a game-changer. I pray that you understand and learn to apply these ideas within your own life. God willing, pass these onto your children and others around you for years to come.

Prologue:

It's taken me over thirty years to get these ideas on paper. A lot has changed in that time. I have come to realize that my entire career path has prepared me for this time in history. The last twenty years of designing and developing adult learning material for corporate clients has provided the skills, insight and necessary experience to design this instructional guide and outline these five mental skills in a way that can be understood and taught. There is so much more to share, God willing more books and discussions will follow. I am excited about this time in history and adding value to others.

Chapter Index:

8. Alonzo Goes to Nebraska

8.1. Guiding Principle: Conditioning & Motivation

8.2. Working Notes:

    8.2.1. Assignment #1 – Re-Conditioning

    8.2.2. Assignment #2 – Daily Achievement

9. Mental Skill #4 – Discrimination

9.1. Guiding Principles:

    9.1.1. Who is responsible

    9.1.2. Window of the future

    9.1.3. 80/20 Rule

10. Mental Skill #5 – Innovation

10.1. Guiding Principle:

    10.1.1. Innovate

    10.1.2. Two Questions

    10.1.3. Performance Improvement

    10.1.4. It's Possible

11. Stress verse Distress

11.1. Movie Scene: Peaceful Warrior

11.2. Guiding Principles:

    11.2.1. Imagination rules

    11.2.2. Vivid Images

    11.2.3. Filters

11.3. Exercise: Reflection #2

11.4. Guiding Principle:

    11.4.1. Personal Agenda

Chapter 1

Introduction

This book is dedicated to understanding the chatter in your head. We have new technology teaching us wonderful new truths that can help us make sense out of so many things like thoughts, emotions and behavior. What we know now is a game-changer in the athletic competition.

Today in the world of sports, we no longer live in a physical economy where physical strength dominates. We now live in a mental economy where what you know and apply on demand dominates the game. This "mental strength" is the new definition of strong. Learning to regulate the chatter and inner dialogue from within is the key to developing this mental strength.

In comparison to physical strength and conditioning, mental training is very similar. Physical strength and conditioning require discipline and a strict daily regimen. You must also create a strict mental regimen for your inner dialogue. Physical attributes will be lost without discipline. Mental skills and ability would be lost enabling the chatter to run rapid and toxic. Now, we are taking the brain into the weight room with mental strength and conditioning. This book is designed to be that workout guide for building your mental strength over time.

Throughout this book you will find good ideas. Guiding principles are what we call "nuggets". A simple idea you can use when working to understand complicated subjects. If this book serves you well, you must continue to seek out new ideas on these topics of thoughts and emotions. As it pertains to your talents and your life long journey of developing your skills and ability, this is only the beginning for you. There is so much more we are learning about the brain and how thoughts and emotions drive performance.

Although this book is primarily about mental skills and regulating your inner chatter, you are wise to understand the connection between thoughts and your emotions. These two are connected at the hip. It's difficult to talk about one without referencing the other. They are independent, and yet directly connected.

"Your thoughts and the chatter in your head directly determine your emotional state."

These two are so subtle it's easy to miss their individual impact on your performance. Your internal dialogue directly affects your emotional states; your emotional states directly affect your decision-making.

Your decision-making is directly affecting your performance. The stakes go up once your realize the chatter is IN-directly affecting your performance.

Understand the process. Your ability to develop Mental Skills to regulate the chatter will directly affect your emotional states. The right emotional state for the task empowers effective decision making, in the moment. Your ability to summon your talents on demand relies on this critical development of better understanding your own thoughts and emotions.

The instruction and ideas in this book will aid you in the first step of development referred to as "awareness", self-awareness to your own personal thoughts. As you grow your mental skills, you learn to regulate your thoughts and in turn learning to regulate negative emotions. The chatter and the emotional state of anxiety are the primary culprit of bad behavior and poor performance. As you develop these mental skills you will in turn learn more about your own talents and ability to play the game at a new level and more importantly, adapt to the pressure on the field and every day life.

Chapter 2

History & Science:

"Our motive is to better understand how we have arrived here today with a new reality of how thoughts and emotions affect performance."

When you talk about mental skills, we are dealing directly with the chatter in your head. Talking with someone about this chatter can be qualified as a very rare conversation. It's not something we used to talk about between two people, sharing this inner dialogue. Only recently, within the last few years have we understood the need to recognize and talk about the chatter. In the past, you were left to figure out on your own.

At some point in sports competition, we've all heard it's a mental game. If your experience is like most, there is not much that follows in the way of "how to" or what that really means. At this point in history we are starting to figure some things out. Based on these new revealed truths we can now teach the mental game and begin to develop these critical thinking skills.

Our curiosity to study the mind and emotions date back to before the times of Jesus Christ; our understanding of these two, however, have just recently reached new depths due to advances in medical technology.

"The brain is the most complicated mass known to man; we have just recently come out of the stone-age in our ability to understand what goes on in the brain."

National Geographic 2013 "The Brain"

It's been said that in order for you to become who you are today, (2nd) and grasp all your potential for tomorrow (3rd), you must learn to understand where you've come from (1st). Notice the numbers and the order in which you are to seek out and understand your journey.

We can apply this same strategy to what we have recently discovered about your brain. With new advancing technology, we can see things like never before. In the last few years, we have confirmed so many working theories from history we can now build on these for the future. This book, its content, and all my efforts to teach and simplify the complex study of "thoughts" and "emotions" become timely in history as we embrace the new realities and move forward learning how to apply what we now know.

2.1 Timeline: Notable Milestones

We can reflect back before the birth of Jesus Christ and see mankind's fascination with thoughts and emotions. There are many notable 'highlights' on the time line in history. The nugget here is to learn your history, to better understand how we have arrived here today. One significant milestone of interest can be found from a book written in the 1920's titled, "Emotions of Normal People" written by William Moulton Marston. This book from Marston and its content laid the foundation for later studies conducted by universities and other research groups. In the mid 1970's, our academic universities picked up on Marston's work and began the study of personality styles.

Understanding different personality styles is another quality study you are recommended to complete. The science of personality traits has evolved with such accuracy it's almost scary to complete a profile and learn how true the assessments can be. This study is an excellent resource to determine your unique, dynamic and organized set of personal traits and patterns of behavior. In short, you learn insights to your own strengths and weaknesses. If you graduate from these early lessons of understanding your own personality style, you then develop skills to better understand the personality styles of others, including the difficult ones.

We include personality style profiling in the "Mental & Emotional Training" program. The D.I.S.C. personality profile is just one of many that has the ability to identify common patterns of weakness; we can pinpoint specific development strategies using the five mental skills from this book, coupled with the summary from a personality profile. It is safe to say the five mental skills and learning the personality styles go hand and hand in your life-long development.

It was in the 1990's, another twenty years later, Dr. Daniel Goleman wrote a book introducing a new theory called "Emotional Intelligence". You can break down the two words and begin to get an idea of the basic principle. "Emotional" references emotions or feelings and "intelligence", meaning smart. In short, how smart are you about your emotions.

One dominant message with "Emotional Intelligence" is the skill sets are learned behaviors. This is so critically important in your development. This science, proven and valid, suggests that you can learn behaviors that make you smarter, more intelligent about your emotions. If you are smarter, more intelligent about your emotions, you in turn make better decisions. When you add a little pressure from the game or in life, your ability to remain smart about your emotions can really benefit your performance.

A high level of emotional intelligence results in good decisions, learning, innovation, adaptability and so many other enabling qualities. Whereas, a low level of emotional intelligence has been proven to result in poor decision-making, hindered learning, lack of flexibility, a lack of adapting and a number of other disabling qualities.

This is such a significant milestone in breaking down the walls and actually talking about how thoughts and emotions go hand in hand with your performance. For the first time in history, science has begun to validate the important role both thoughts and emotions play in your day-to-day decision-making. Since these learned behaviors improve decision-making, we can now develop instructional guides and lesson plans to teach mental and emotional skill development. They may be considered soft-skills when compared to more "technical skills" required for a specific job or task. However, the soft-skill sets are now proven to play as big of a roll, if not bigger, than the technical skills. For so long, the idea of mental and emotional conversations has been categorized as motivational or a warm fuzzy pep rally. Now, there are identifiable mental and emotional skill sets that we must learn, practice and teach.

Dr. Goleman's work has since expanded and many others have now taken the concept of "Emotional Intelligence" and begun to explore all the possibilities. Our academic models from kindergarten through High School and our universities are now including courses supporting the ideas of Emotional Intelligence. Here is where you receive encouragement to go and talk with your counselor about Emotional Intelligence courses; go find a good book on the subject and learn these valuable new behaviors.

Mental: "Learning to regulate the chatter" 18

As it pertains to new technology, Neuroscience is the field of study revealing these groundbreaking ideas about thoughts and emotions. Neuroscience is the study of the nervous system. An "inter-disciplinary" approach combining psychology, biology, physiology and so many other disciplines it's like a melting pot of all the knowledge and what we have learned up to this time in history.

Here is where we take the traditional sports psychology models and tweak with new factual insights about how the mind and body work together.

When we take the combined knowledge of science and couple it with advancing medical technology we can see things in your brain like never before. For the first time in history, we can study the nervous system. We can see your brain think. We can now study a brain with desire. We can monitor and learn how your brain interacts with another brain during a normal conversation. This new and exciting field of study is a game-changer and it's called Neuroscience.

It's important to understand the relationship between these two because they compliment one another so well. Emotional Intelligence deals directly with you understanding your thoughts and feelings where as Neuroscience is helping us learn and understand the "emotional" brain and what experts in the field call, "emotional brain states".

In 2009 the Journal of Science and Sports Medicine introduced an article titled, "Validity of the Emotional Intelligence Scale for Use in Sports". This was the first notable research on Emotional Intelligence in athletic competition. The research introduced the idea that certain emotions enable better performance whereas other emotions disable and lead to poor performance. A second article released in 2010 highlighted more research offering new findings that emotional states are important for peak performance.

Now, jump to 2011 in ESPN Magazine. The article, "I Think, Therefore, I Choke". A wonderful read with what may be the first mainstream article on how thoughts and emotions can either help you succeed or cause you to fail. The article goes into the "anatomy of a choke". It's another look at how thoughts and emotions affect your game.

Why am I spending time on this history? It is important to understand the recent changes in how we look at your brain; it's happening in your lifetime. It pertains to how we used to think and how we think now. It's a brand new ballgame.

> *"The old thinking, and this really goes back to the '60s and '70s was that, you know, right brain good, left brain bad. Actually, that is very, very outdated. The new-sophisticated thinking is first when it comes to left versus right you mean left front, left middle, left rear. And when it comes to creativity it's not just left 'or' right, it's up 'or' down. It's the whole brain. And here it's important to understand the structural difference between the right hemisphere and the left hemisphere."*
>
> The Latest Findings On The Brain

What he is basically saying is your brain is very complex. So complex we've only started to scratch the surface on what we are learning about your emotional brain-states. What you must learn to understand is the way we used to think about the brains role in your performance has changed. We now know that if you can learn to increase your awareness to your thoughts, then learn to regulate your thoughts you can empower yourself to do amazing things.

Dr. Goleman goes on to say,

> "Self-awareness and self-regulation, these are the basis for self-mastery of all kinds. These are the abilities that make someone, for example, an outstanding individual performer and a star on their own. It has to do with awareness of our internal states, accessing those states and mastery of those states."

If you are a top performer, you have learned how to regulate emotional states. By regulating your chatter, you in turn regulate the body's emotional response to the situation or task at hand. My interest is in you understanding these ideas so well you learn to summon these talents on demand. Your knowledge and understanding of these skills can now be taught and it is part of your responsibility to develop your mental strength and conditioning.

Show me a top performer in your game, somebody you love to watch. This athlete, like you, has a "mental fingerprint" in the brain for every task performed. In theory, we can teach you how to study your 'fingerprint' by looking at the thoughts and emotions when executing a task. The idea is for you to learn to map the emotional states that lead you to extraordinary performance. Once you can understand these ideas and learn to map your mental fingerprint, you then capture it, study it, call it up on demand and with skill development duplicate it on often. And it all starts with the chatter in your head.

2.2.1 Guiding Principle: Two brains

Here is a simple idea for a complicated topic. Let's pretend for a minute that you have two brains, a thinking brain and a feeling brain (not really, this is just an example). The feeling brain can take over the thinking brain.

It's very similar to a master-slave relationship; the feeling brain being the master, the thinking brain being the slave. When this happens, we call this an emotional highjack. Remember these words, emotional highjack. We will cover more on this later. This becomes important because when the feeling brain takes over the thinking brain, it takes mental skills to recover. The stronger the skill set, the quicker the recovery. The weaker the skill set, the slower recovery.

In other words, if your chatter continues to be negative, you literally stay in an emotional highjack. Your emotional states are causing all kinds of negative and distracting feelings. Your body releases dopamine, adrenaline, cortisol and several other stress hormones into your body. The root cause is your chatter, often referred to as attitude. The constant negative, toxic chatter runs rampant directly affecting your emotional states that in turn dump stress hormones into your system. Not good.

Understanding your thoughts and emotions can be complicated; all the more reason to get started on mastering these mental skills right now. My ability to put words together and simplify is only the beginning. Once you know and understand the process, you must then go to work on the inside, applying new disciplines to grow and strengthen your mental muscle.

This book and the attempts to make these topics simple are my talents put into action. I can take these complicated truths and ideas, break them down for you and make them user friendly so you can begin to apply these ideas into your day-to-day chatter. If there is one thing that you can learn to develop and pay closer attention to is the chatter in your own head.

This is your development goal. Step one, become more aware of your inner dialogue. This is your first step. As you become more aware, you begin to regulate the chatter, step two. It's that simple, you can do this.

The ancient scriptures talk about taking that chatter captive and renewing it often. When you consider all that is at stake, your future, your dreams and your desires. And you recognize how real and relevant the threat of failure really is, your new goal is to take captive and renew your chatter 86,400 seconds of every day.

2.2.2 Guiding Principle: It's complicated

The mind is complicated. Thoughts are complicated. Thoughts pop up in your head sometimes and only God knows from where they come. You can be sitting in class or in a meeting; someone or something distracts you. Too much, too little, too loud, you know all the distractions. All of the sudden, your mind takes off like a racehorse. Random thoughts pop up and not one of them belong in your head. Unexpected emotions and feelings will follow. You must learn to develop new skills to regulate thoughts and in turn regulating emotions so they do not distract you; accept this is difficult and requires your daily discipline.

As a basic truth, your chatter continues 24 hours a day, 7 days a week. This is equal to 1440 minutes; it's the same day and same amount of time just broken down in more detail. Your brain works faster than that and so does your chatter. In the same twenty-four hour day you must develop your awareness to the chatter at the seconds level, 86,400 seconds of every day. You must develop the mental skills to become more aware and pay closer attention second by second.

There is no shutting off the chatter, only awareness and regulation. You have thoughts, which is mental. You have feelings, which is emotional. You have action, which is physical. In this book, you will learn how the chatter impacts them all. You really cannot talk about one without referencing the other two. Again, these conversations about your inner dialogue are new and when introduced for the first time can be a little complicated. This is where my gift, my strength, my service comes into play. My role is to take these complicated truths and introduce simple ideas enabling these truths to be user-friendly so that you can take action, right here, right now, today.

2.2.3 Guiding Principle: T.E.A.

Here is a quick reference to remind your self often, T.E.A.:

Mental: "Learning to regulate the chatter"

Thoughts = **E**motions = **A**ction

This book is dedicated to understanding the "T", your thoughts (thinking). What you must learn to understand and accept is whatever thoughts you allow will determine your emotions, in turn driving your actions. Your feelings and emotional state ultimately determine how you handle yourself on and off the field and all areas of life.

Chapter 3

Mental Skill #1:

Communication

Definition: "The ability to select the <u>right</u> words and

<u>right</u> mental pictures; on demand"

When we say the mental skill of "communication", we are referring to the mind and what goes on inside of your head. Specifically, we are referencing your self-talk. You engaged in the act of talking to your self.

3.1.1 Guiding Principle: Outside versus inside

Outside is our communication with others; what we traditionally think when we reference communication. It's a conversation you have with your teammate, your spouse, your kids, your friend or neighbor. You must filter words from others, yes. But more importantly, you must filter your words on the inside as well. Learn to have healthy conversations with yourself.

Science will teach you about a part of the brain called the prefrontal cortex. We are just now learning so much more about this area in the brain and the critically important roll it plays in your thinking throughout the day. The prefrontal cortex is located right behind your forehead. It is always on, always thinking, always flashing words and mental pictures.

Some experts have referred to this area of the brain as the "good boss". This "good boss" title implies two things. One, it's good in the way it helps you with decision-making, problem solving, over coming challenges and conflicts. The second is that it plays a very powerful roll to seeking out threats and difficulty. When the "good boss" finds a threat from your past, present or your future, it can set off the alarm system in the "bad boss". The "bad boss" is referred to as the feeling brain and the alarm system is that emotional highjack we spoke of earlier. If you remember, during a highjack your decision-making, your learning and ability to innovate and adapt is all hindered. When the "bad boss" is in charge, your body is flooded with stress hormones that if not managed properly will begin to work against you and your performance. Remember, it is your ability to flex these mental skills that empower you to recover and get the "good boss" back in charge.

Learning to become more aware of the chatter and learning to regulate the chatter is the foundation of the first mental skill. The mental skill of communication is your ability to place the <u>right</u> words and the <u>right</u> mental pictures supporting your dreams, goals and desires. This skill level is demonstrated in your ability to regulate the chatter using the right words and right mental pictures on demand and in the moment.

3.1.2 Guiding Principle: Words and Mental Pictures

You have random words and mental pictures flashing throughout the day and night without any conscious effort from you. When you're thinking or simply letting your mind wander, words and mental pictures flash though your brain. When I ask, *"What's on your mind"*? Words and mental pictures will instantly appear and these will be what you describe in your answer. If I say, *"do you remember the time..."* you will pull up stored words and mental pictures. If I say, "imagine yourself in competition tomorrow" words and mental pictures will be what you describe. Chatter, self-talk is simply a series of random words and mental pictures. This guiding principle is a critical step in learning the five mental skills.

As you journey through each day, you will now begin to pay attention to your words and mental pictures. Basically you are paying closer attention to your self-talk or chatter. As you improve your awareness, gradually and with practice you will learn to flex this mental skill and regulate the words and mental pictures. This act of regulating is simply replacing the bad chatter with good chatter. You are learning to take the bad chatter out and place good chatter in.

The key is to remember the chatter is running without your awareness and without your efforts to regulate. As you will learn later, most of the chatter is working against you. Most of the words and mental pictures which flash randomly in your head will tend to be negative, minor and without real reasons to even keep in your chatter. Unaware and unregulated chatter will hold you back from achieving your dreams and your desires.

3.1.3 Guiding Principle: Negative by Design

Knowing the chatter never stops, understand it will most often seek the negative, the wrong or the threat, and it does so by design. One of the many functions of your brain is to protect. It is very similar to a security system keeping the body safe and out of harm's way.

This negative bias is another critical understanding moving forward in your development. You must seek to understand this basic negative nature. A critical lesson here is to recognize this negative bias may often set off "false-alarms" in your chatter. Your chatter will "run away" and you will start thinking about all kinds of different scenarios. This is what I call "chasing cats" or basically wasting time, talent and energy on pity chatter (thoughts that just do not matter). Your chatter takes you down a road of different situations and circumstances that have nothing to do with the truth and that moment in time. You un-intentionally focus on words and mental pictures that have very little relevance to what is important and in turn, hinder your achievement. By learning to accept this truth you begin navigating the journey and overcoming the harmful affects of un-regulated chatter. Chatter that simply doesn't belong.

Your words and mental pictures will tend to focus more on what's wrong and who's to blame; more on the easy than the hard; more on hurting emotions rather than rational logic. It's a constant awareness you must work to regulate. The mental skill of communication has everything to do with your awareness and regulation of the chatter, disciplining the right words and right mental pictures on demand.

3.2 Movie Scene: Devil's Advocate

Under pressure is when these mental skills and ability serve you the best. Here is a great scene in the movie Devil's Advocate to illustrate your talent in the face of pressure. In this scene we find Keanu Reeves and Al Pacino, the two are talking while they walk on top of a high-rise building in downtown New York. This scene is so relevant to your situation you can really bridge the gap between knowing this skill and learning to apply it in daily life.

Imagine yourself in this scene as Reeves and Pacino is your coach or recruiter:

Reeves: *"You offering me a job?"*

Pacino: *"I'm thinking about it. I know you got talent. I knew that before you got here. It's just the other thing, I wonder about."*

Reeves: *"What thing is that?"*

Pacino: *"Pressure. Changes everything, pressure. Some people you squeeze them and they focus, others fold. Can you summon your talent at will? Can you deliver on a deadline? Can you sleep at night?"*

Translation, can you regulate the chatter? Can you regulate the words and mental pictures even under pressure? Can you recover from toxic self-talk and re-gain your composure? It's a skill. It's your ability and the secret lies inside your chatter.

What you will come to learn and understand is that most of what's happening outside of you is uncontrollable. The focus need be on the inside, starting with your thoughts. At any given moment, any given situation throughout the day, what matters most is right here, right now and what's going on in your mind. You can learn to develop day in and day out, knowing good and well that pressure awaits. You must learn and develop these skills sets daily and throughout the day knowing that the pressure points await around every corner or next new play.

"The last place to learn CPR is at the scene of an accident; learn it first and practice often for the time in need and on demand."

3.3.1 Guiding Principle: Truth vs. Opinion

What you are seeking in the chatter is truth. When you learn to be aware and regulate your self-talk, you must seek truth verses opinion.

Beware of opinions. Opinions are not always true; your opinions and those opinions of others must be refined before you allow them to hang out in your chatter for too long. A lot of times your chatter, as you well know, will be like a repetitive gong of trashy words and mental pictures that do not belong. The chatter will have you all over the road thinking about different kinds of stuff, most of which is hurting you and has no relevance. Seek the truth in your mind, defining words and mental pictures that reveal what is true.

3.3.2 Guiding Principle: Mental Recorder

This is another separate class by itself and a worthy study, the subconscious mind. It is important to know and understand that as you are sitting here right now, your chatter is running. Every word, every mental picture is being recorded. You have your own internal mental recorder that captures every second of the day.

So let me ask you, what words and mental pictures do you allow to be recorded?

Beware! The recorder doesn't judge or filter for truth. It only captures what you allow in the chatter, true or not. Everyone outside can be applauding you saying, *"great job",* but in your mind, if you are beating yourself up, that's the dominant message and that is what your recorder captures. More importantly, this detail is how your brain prepares for your next performance.

You must learn to regulate the chatter today, in turn programming the recorder for the next performance. You must learn to pump positive thoughts into your mind, positive words and mental pictures of how you desire things to be. Your recorder will capture it, and in a simplified process, prepares you for the next opportunity. This is the process of skill development over time.

You must remember and accept as truth, your subconscious mind doesn't judge or sensor your chatter. The recorder just captures it. There is no good word or bad word buzzer that goes off, no sense of a good or bad mental picture. The mental recorder does not censor if your chatter is true or false, beneficial or harmful. This is where you mental skills come into play when regulating.

When you take on the discipline to be aware and regulate the chatter, you force-feed the mental recorder 86,400 seconds of every day. You take your goals, your desires, your ambitions and engineer specific words and mental pictures to achieve such things, and think on them as often as possible.

When you are pumping the weight getting bigger, better and stronger you are now regulating the chatter at the same time. When you are running plays and working on the physical fundamentals you are executing the task a thousand times over and now you are regulating the mental at the same time. If in your chatter you neglect to flex this mental-muscle your most primitive emotions will surface under pressure: fear, doubt and rage.

You know better than I all the trashy chatter that pops up, if you're not dealing with this in your own inner words and mental pictures, in the critical moment of a real competition, you will increase the odds of failure and fall to the one that does.

3.3.3 Guiding Principle: Nourish & Fight

When it comes to regulating your chatter and using your mental skill of communication, you must learn to nourish like a mother and fight like a father. You must nourish with good words and mental pictures; you must fight the bad ones.

Two agendas when it comes to, "Hey, what does it look like acting on this mental skill of communication?"

It looks like you sitting right here, right now, when you leave here, when you're sitting in you're vehicle, sitting on the toilet, taking a shower, any and everywhere, all day long learning to nourish and fight the chatter. It's a daily thing. No matter where you are throughout the day, your chatter is running and all of the sudden you're going to find yourself critical and beating yourself up. You are going to be more aware and regulate by flexing this mental skill of communication and replace the negative toxic chatter with nourishing words and mental pictures.

You must work to discipline yourself and regulate the chatter. You must put negative words and mental pictures in a corner or they will put you in a corner of doubt and indecision. It's like a mad dog in the house; you will remain in doubt and fear, always hesitating, never clear and forever lacking confidence. You must capture the negative words and pictures as if a father saying to an enemy, *come closer and you will cease to exist!* Every time you capture this chatter and regulate it, you are flexing the mental muscle. You are fighting to defend what is near and dear to you, and only you can learn to carry on this fight.

"The fight is internal, battling within you, both good and bad battling to control one thing, your chatter"

When it comes to nourishing like a mother, you must learn to talk nicely to yourself. You must put good words and good mental pictures in your chatter. Learn to rely on yourself as the primary provider for the nourishing words and mental pictures you need. In the study of emotional intelligence, we call this "self-reliance". This is where you learn to rely on your own words and mental pictures rather than relying on others around.

Yes, we need words and positive influence from those around us, yes! Yes, it is always nice to hear it from a coach. There is no debate here; even the scriptures validate the notion of fellowship and two becoming stronger than one. However, don't rely on the external folks as your primary source. You must play the primary role for your own personal nourishment. Do not rely solely on your coach, your family member or someone else outside of you. You do it. It's your discipline, your gift and your promise for the future. When I say, *"Nourish like a mother,"* you must find times in your 86-4 (short for 86,400 seconds) when you're saying, *"I can, I will, I see, I know, it's coming, it's possible."*

Sometimes you must learn to muster-up the courage to find new words and mental pictures which face your fears. Truth be told, your next great achievement hasn't happened yet; you've yet to experience it. You can experience it in the mind with disciplined chatter and the courage to see yourself winning. A strong mental skill of communication will slowly nourish and condition your beliefs building confidence and self-esteem.

You must first believe it for yourself using the right words and right mental pictures in your chatter. You are going to have to use words and mental images that are new to you when you visualize your next achievements. You must learn to "see" yourself beyond your circumstances with new words and mental pictures. We will talk more about this need for new chatter later in the book.

As a wise point of reference, the scriptures teach to think on whatever is kind, loving, true and honorable. These are your new guidelines for filtering (regulating) your chatter.

3.3.4 Guiding Principle: Conditioning

Your chatter, randomly wandering each second of the day, is captured into your mental recorder. Over time, as the chatter runs rampant and always being recorded, the dominant words and mental pictures create connections in the brain. We call this conditioning, where the connections create habits and are formed by repetitive thoughts. Your attitude for example is often the result of repetitive chatter over time. In our skill development we learn that attitude is nothing more than a habit of thinking. A habit that has been created and conditioned based on your chatter.

The dominant words and mental pictures are those that you repeat over and over again in the chatter, called repetitive thought. These dominant impressions from your chatter impact your own personal beliefs and challenge your own personal value. Before you know it, you've conditioned yourself to act and respond based on random chatter that does not support your dreams or desires.

It is important to understand how conditioning works to affect your skills, confidence, and self-esteem. Conditioning even affects how you manage your relationships. We now understand how the chatter can condition positively and negatively. It all depends on you and your chatter.

By learning to develop and understand this truth on conditioning you can use it to your advantage. By regulating the chatter with specific words and mental pictures of good performance, you are conditioning. In other words, during the 86,400 seconds of your day, chatter is running, the recorder is capturing. You must learn to condition yourself to make more mature decisions based on what's going on in your chatter.

3.3.5 Guiding Principle: The "Fish Tank" Promise

A wise mentor shared this story with me over twenty years ago. This will help you understand the process you are starting as you learn to regulate and apply these new mental skills.

Imagine a large fish tank filled with coffee. This dingy, dark looking water is the result of poor conditioning over time, allowing the chatter to run rampant and unregulated. We've all been poorly programmed by allowing negative, unworthy chatter to run rampant, making false and toxic impressions.

Now, imagine a hose of fresh, clear running water and you put it into the fish tank, leaving it over time. What happens to the dark, dingy water? With continued effort of fresh water coming in, the dingy water is out and the new clear water fills the tank.

As you continue seeking new insights and learning to flex your mental skills, refining your chatter is the fresh, clear running water. You are the hose and you are putting new words and new mental pictures into the mental fish tank, reprogramming and reconditioning from within. This takes time and discipline and it's reserved for only the few willing to look inside.

Chapter 4

Skills & Ability

"This book is an instructional guide to learning and developing your mental skills. This is not a motivational speech or pep rally."

It is too easy to overlook the pain, the disciplines, and the suffering required to refine this mental skill set. Mental skills are like every other skill; you must work and discipline your self to develop. Referring to these mental and emotional skills as simple motivation is to deny your own personal intellect and discount the thinking power and ability of your brain. It is your intellect that places you higher on the food chain. It is your ability to feel emotions that make you unique unlike any other creator on earth. Learning how to use this intellect in regulating emotions can be one of the most beneficial skills you will ever learn.

The good news, you're already using these five mental skills already, though probably not very well, and as a result your emotions affect your decision-making. All we want to do is learn to become more aware of these mental skills, which in turn empower us to regulate the chatter.

In Dr. John Maxwell's "21 Irrefutable Laws of Leadership", we learn about the "Law of the Process". This leadership law is defined as, "develop daily, not in a day". This law helps us better understand the new journey you are on by learning to take thoughts and emotions captive. Everyday you will practice new levels of awareness to your inner thoughts. The fact we now have a science to confirm these skills, we can now assign responsibility. In other words, you are responsible for your inner thoughts and you will be amazed with your results once you learn to regulate.

The definition of "skill" is the ability to do something well. In sports competition, you must do it well and do it on demand and in the moment when the need arises. On a scale from one to ten for example, you may be a four on the skill metrics, with work you can improve. This is a natural development journey and one you are encouraged to take by applying these ideas in this book.

The new reality of sports competition however, requires the skill and ability in all three domains, physical, mental and emotional. The new-strong stay to play, while the mental and emotionally weak go home. Here is where developing physical and mental strength training goes hand in hand. It's not just about practicing the physical game; you must now learn to develop the mental and emotional skills while practicing the physical game. In the new reality of today those who have the mental skills and ability to deliver under pressure are those that make the cut. Those that do not or have not yet developed this mental strength simply choke, end early and go home, frustrated.

Only a few get to dress, wear the uniform, and take the field of play. These are the ones that have developed the mental, physical and emotional skill-sets.

4.1.1 Guiding Principle: Transferable

At some point you will begin to understand these five skills are transferable. Yes, they're going to help you in the game and in competition. They will also help you in the classroom and other domains in your life.

My greatest success story on this lesson is from a young man named Alonzo Moore. Alonzo was a 2011 graduate from Winnfield High School; we first met during his sophomore summer. He is a great example of how the mental muscle on the field, when recognized and regulated, can be transferred into the classroom. The same five skills Alonzo used on the field to earn a full ride football scholarship; he took into the classroom for even greater achievements. Now, as a result, he excels academically with the same success and consistency he does athletically.

"Think neither victory or defeat, think only on execution"

Dr. Jeff Garrison

4.2.1 Guiding Principle: 86,400 (86-4)

We have twenty-four hours in this day. The same amount of time broken down into minutes equals one thousand, four hundred and forty. Go one-step further, the same amount of time, broken down into seconds will equal eighty six thousand four hundred. What's my point? It is at the *seconds* level that you need to learn awareness and regulation. We call this constant engagement of your skill sets. You will learn to flex this mental muscle on demand in the same way you would expect your body to flex and support you on a task.

Depending on what book you read, some psychologists will say it's a one-to-one. For every second on the clock there is an internal conversation in your head. Even while sleeping, your subconscious chatter is still running. At times, the chatter often leaves the imprint of dreams you remember when you wake up. New science has proven that the average person engages in self-talk, the inner dialogue, at a rate of 300 to 1000 words a minute. This translates into 5 to 16 words a second!

Take this truth of fast, rambling chatter and consider another truth. The mind only holds one thought at a time. This is a lesson by itself. The mind thinks faster than what you can keep track in your cognitive thinking. The chatter (self-talk) is so fast that you can be sitting here reading this book and flashing back to earlier events in the day and still comprehends what you are reading. It appears like you are able to have multiple thoughts at the same time. Please, do not be misled science validates this truth, only one thought at a time. Even when multi-tasking, your brain holds one thought and is capable of shuffling these thoughts at pace faster than we can track or keep up.

Now, the million-dollar question, how much of your chatter is in your favor? How many of those thoughts flashing randomly through your head today are positive and respectful, encourage hope and optimism, inspire personal motivation and action, or help you navigate the known disruptive thoughts and emotional distractions?

"Are you talking to yourself with the utmost respect?"

How much of these internal thoughts, just from today, are beating you up? Here is where awareness is critically important and you begin to work on your self and regulating your chatter. We call this negative, toxic chatter, self-criticism. Allowing your chatter to remain unregulated is immature at best and this critical voice becomes an internal enemy. The mature, through skill development, learn to regulate the wandering thoughts and focus on self-evaluation rather than self-criticism. There is a big difference in your chatter when it comes to your personal performance and delivering results under pressure.

You can better understand this subtle, yet critical step in evaluating your thoughts when you learn more about the many roles your brain plays every day. Many of these roles we often take fore granted. One such role the brain plays is to protect you. It is very similar to a "security system". That mass between your ears, one of the most complex things ever known to man, is pre-programmed to seek out the negative and find what went wrong. As you grow in awareness, you will find your chatter seeking, searching, replaying and pre-playing the threats and looking at what went wrong or what could go wrong in the future. And all of this goes on in your chatter with no effort from you.

4.3.1 Guiding Principle: Weeds

Just like the weeds in the garden, negative chatter grows on its own; it does not require your attention. You do not need to nourish these negative thoughts, like the weeds in the garden, the negativity in your self-talk will grow on it's own.

Get over the idea your thoughts are going to be negative, you need not remain immature and struggle with this truth. It's going to happen. It's okay. You must take your inner dialogue captive; you must learn and grow your mental skills and practice these skills often. It is a discipline of the mind. It sounds simple. It is and you can do this. Always remember, what is simple is not always easy.

The same is true for nourishing the good thoughts. Similar to the garden you must nourish what is good in you; you must also learn to nourish good thoughts. The short story in this new journey is that you must learn to get both done, fight and nourish the chatter. Based on what you want to achieve and the feelings you wish to embrace, you must nourish the good chatter and draw on the positive and in the same way you must weed the negative chatter.

We can break these ideas of thoughts and emotions down to where it's simple to know and understand. The real challenge comes when you start to apply these ideas day to day. When you're out in your 86,400 seconds of the day and the pressure mounts, the stakes go up. You engage in competition or conflict. When there is real and relevant risk and you are going to lose something, maybe your job or position. When you are not making the grade and it's all on the line. When the opposite sex seeks to distract you. When your brain chases lust and disruptive thoughts and emotions. These are the defined times when you must learn to apply your new mental skills. Your test is coming; it is part of the set up in life. When the stakes go up, if you are not right in your daily chatter a choke awaits.

"Tomorrow's performance is determined by today's chatter."

Your next performance, whether it's going to school and taking a test or going to practice to take your position, it all starts with regulating your chatter.

Chapter 5

Mental Skill #2:

Concentration

Definition: "The ability to <u>repeat</u> <u>specific</u> words and <u>specific</u> mental pictures; on demand"

The second mental skill is concentration. I admit, when I first learned this skill back in the mid 90's, I did not know that concentrating could be defined as a skill or ability.

Remember, this is a mental ability. Everything we talk about refers to the words and mental pictures you allow in your thoughts. When we talk about concentration, we're talking about your ability to pick specific words and mental pictures and keep them in your thoughts for extended periods of time.

5.1.1 Guiding Principle: Wandering chatter

Your mind will always wander away from that which you are specifically trying to focus. Seek understanding on this truth and do not struggle with it. For example, you focus and concentrate on item "A" and before you know it, your thoughts wander and you find yourself thinking about "X, Y and Z". This is normal. In fact, every time you bring your chatter back to the original item "A", it's the same as a rep when weightlifting or physical training. Recognize that every time your chatter drifts and you're able to bring it back to your main idea is a good thing. This is when you are flexing, strengthening, and conditioning your mental skill of concentration.

There are many studies on attention disorders and supporting research to validate such a condition. However, you must learn to concentrate and do so on demand just like every other athlete. You must arrive with competitive results if you expect to compete, and concentration, regulating the chatter and keeping it focused is one key component. If you have a pre-existing condition and you struggle to stay focused, bottom line is that you must work harder, smarter. You must learn to develop this mental skill on demand in order to produce desired results. If you have to work a little harder than the one next to you, so be it.

5.1.2 Guiding Principle: Common Senses

God gave you five common senses: Sight, sound, taste, touch and smell. You go through every second of your day gathering data from these five common senses. It's called sensory perception: Data comes in, your chatter defines it and your brain stores it by creating connections.

5.2 Movie Scene: For the Love of the Game

There is a classic scene in this movie with Kevin Costner who stars as a baseball legend hanging on for one more game. In this scene Costner gives one of the greatest lines of all time, *"clear the mechanism"*.

Costner is on the mound, the fans are mocking him, the horns are blaring, each one of his five senses are on a mega-overload with hundreds of distractions. If you are a competitive athlete you understand this moment, you've been here before.

Then you hear it, *"clear the mechanism"*. At that moment in the movie the sound goes off, literally. You start thinking that something is wrong with your television. Then, all of the sudden, visually everything on the screen is blurred accept Costner's character. The next thing you see is the batter standing in the box and everything is blurred except for the batter. What an excellent example of what you are now learning to do in developing your mental skill of concentration. You are learning to clear the mechanism, to turn down the sensory perception, and focus on the task at hand with specific words and mental pictures.

5.3.1 Guiding Principle: Your Words

Create your own set of specific words and mental pictures to engage your talent. You must define and refine the specific words and mental pictures for a specific task. Be sure to make the words short, not a lot of words or a long story. And be sure to make the mental pictures very clear and vivid. When actually executing a task, your mind does not do well with general words and casual mental pictures. Create your word and mental picture list and be very specific so you can repeat often with self-discipline in your chatter.

Costner's character used *"clear the mechanism"*. Find your own and create many for different words and mental pictures that support your task. Most importantly, learn how to turn down the volume on your common senses. When you develop these mental skills and learn to lower the volume on your sensory perception your ability to focus on the task at hand improves. Rather than allowing your sensory perception to overload your chatter and run rampant you are able to prioritize your thoughts in that moment. This is an act of concentrating on your pre-defined thoughts (your specific words and mental pictures you've already defined) rather than the data from your common senses.

5.3.2 Guiding Principle: Can you sleep?

Controlled breathing is key to relaxing the body and your muscles. Meditation is a powerful tool that uses your mental skills in order to control body function. One way I have learned to practice this in my chatter is to focus on specific muscles such as my heart and lungs. Visualize mental pictures of your muscles. I went out and found pictures of all the muscles in the body. I looked in books, the Internet, even posters from my doctor's office. I pull up these mental pictures from memory (connections) as I fall asleep, still amped from events that happened earlier in the day, or the movie I just watched. You must learn to understand how much power and control you have on your body functions by developing your mental skills and regulating the chatter.

Regulate, repeat and focus your chatter in your favor. You now have specific words and specific mental pictures you use to communicate with yourself, disciplined self-talk. You can now take these specific words and mental pictures and concentrate on them, often repeating throughout the day, by design and with purpose. You will drift off in your chatter; simply flex the mental muscle and repeat the specific words and mental pictures again and again.

5.3.3 Guiding Principle: Windows

Human nature is to rewind the game tape and seek out the negative. Your nature is to look through the window of the past and see everything you did wrong. For the sake of instruction and learning to understand how rapid the mind chats, we refer to windows. You have one of three windows you are looking through at any given second of the day. Your thoughts will be looking through the past-window, the present-window or the future-window. By learning the windows and regulating your thoughts accordingly, you can bring structure to your chatter so that it's not so overwhelming at times.

Think back to our earlier conversations about Neuroscience; the study of the nervous system. We have recently learned the mind holds only one thought at a time. It is a truth hard to understand at first. It seems as though we can hold many different words and mental pictures at the same time, multi-tasking for example. Science validates the truth, one thought at a time.

The important lesson here is to understand how amazingly fast the mind runs rampant, flashing these words and mental pictures. It's so fast that we are led to believe it's just a constant rattle, a bombarding cascade of too much and too many thoughts at one time. It's this amazing ability of the chatter to run so fast that we often compare it to a computer or computing power. In this case, all the computing power in the world does not compare to the awesome power between your ears.

To be a top-performing athlete who learns to summon your talent on demand, you train your chatter, no matter which window you are looking through. To put it another way, it doesn't matter if you are thinking about your past, present or future. You discipline your chatter with truth and in your favor. If you find yourself thinking (chatting) through the window of the past, then you must learn how to rewind and do it correctly; chatter in the past, left alone and unregulated, will hurt you.

Today, in this present-window, in this moment, you must learn how to discipline your chatter on what is most important, right here, right now. Chatter in the present-window left alone and unregulated will keep you in a constant feeling of uncertainty, a slave to emotions, and paralysis by analysis.

You might catch yourself thinking about tomorrow or the future, something you have no control over. In the future-window you must learn how to preview coming events in your life. Chatter in the future-window left alone and unregulated will distract you by wasting valuable time by majoring on minor issues and causing you to question yourself, your personal value and your abilities.

5.3.4 Guiding Principle: Window of the Past

The past is perfect; you can't change it. This is one of the harder lessons to learn when developing your mental skills. In regards to this past-window, you must act in courage and in faith, regulate your chatter and seek to understand; seek the do-betters. This is a difficult lesson to teach, and often takes the most time to learn. A top performer understands that when you rewind and reflect back through the past-window there's a right way to do it and a wrong way.

There are two questions you must ask yourself after every task. For example, after an interaction with a family member, your coach, or a competition, you would direct your present chatter to reflect back, asking these two questions.

The first *"what did I do right?"*

This is your "*at-ta-boy*". It is so critically important for you to point out too yourself what was good in your decisions and performance. One of the many important reasons for this reaffirmation is to capture the good in your mental recorder, which in turn prepares you for future performance.

The second question is a trick question. Most, just like you, allow the chatter to focus on *"what did I do wrong?"* You must understand this is critical and is toxic to allow your chatter to run rampant on the wrongdoings. It's harmful and holds you back when your chatter focuses on what went wrong. It's like a curse that connects all the windows. Our lack of understanding how to reflect back correctly in the chatter allows the negative chatter in the present to dominate, in turn hindering future opportunities.

The "disciplined" second question is *"what can I do better?"*

It almost sounds too simple. It's very subtle, yet so critical. Something happens inside of you with your body's stress response system and the way your body responds when you seek the "do-better" rather than the 'done-poorly". You are now using your chatter, with skill & ability, when you reflect back correctly. By doing this often with repetition, you strengthen your mental concentration skill. In short, when you seek the "do-better", it's like looking for where the dominos broke down in the sequence of tasks. You are intentionally seeking to understand where to make small little corrections. The domino exercise is one we use when instructing the "Task Analysis", another great tool for targeting where the chatter need be disciplined for all three windows.

5.4 Natural Law: The Law of Concentration

In learning about the mental skill of concentration, there is also a law. You must learn and understand both the mental skill and the law.

The definition of the law of concentration says, *"You always move in the direction of your dominant thought; what you focus on grows, whatever you think about expands."*

The mental skill of concentration is the ability to regulate the chatter and focus on demand. The law, however, is a natural law. The natural law of concentration can be compared to the law of gravity. We understand the law of gravity exists, we understand there are consequences and benefits to the law. Obey this natural law and reap the benefits, disobey and you will suffer the consequences. Nature holds you accountable.

The same is true with the law of concentration and the chatter in which you repeat often or focus on. If you obey the law of concentration and create disciplined chatter; if you focus often on the right and the "do-betters" you will reap many benefits. If you disobey this law of concentration and allow the chatter to run rampant, out of control from disruptive thoughts and disruptive emotions, you will suffer the consequences, often revealed in poor performance.

If you understand the law and you work it in your favor, there are great benefits. On the down side, the consequences have great disadvantages. Remember, it's a natural law so nature is the judge and the jury on holding you accountable.   Whatever you are thinking about the most becomes your dominant thought. If your chatter is focused on what is wrong, your dominant thought will be wrong. Your mental recorder captures and expands on what you focus on, the wrong.

The mental skill of concentration is the ability to create the right chatter and repeat often. The law of concentration says that whatever chatter you allow most often to repeat, right wrong or indifferent, that specific chatter will grow and pop up even more.

You must learn to force-feed the good; create a library of specific words and mental pictures that support all your dreams and desires in every aspect of your life. Remember, the weeds and negative chatter are going to grow on their own. The bad thoughts, the bad chatter will grow all by itself, it's natural. You do not need to nourish the weeds. You do, however, have to create your library of nourishing words and have mental pictures standing by and ready to pull into the chatter.

5.5.1 Guiding Principle: Enhance the skill

Concentration is a skill. Every skill can be enhanced with practice. In a recent study entitled, "The Latest Findings on the Brain", Emotional Intelligence pioneer Dr. Goleman says,

"Many meditation methods from the Christian

or Jewish tradition, or from Asia, are essential ways of building concentration. The cardinal rule of all concentration enhancement techniques is focus on "A" and to bring it back as soon as you realize your mind has wandered to "B" "C," "D," "E," or "F". It's like being on a weight machine and doing physical reps for a muscle. Every time you bring a wandering mind back to a concentrated state, you're enhancing the muscles of concentration."

5.5.2 Guiding Principle: Optimal Performance

Your development goal is very clear. It's called optimal state or optimal performance. It is a state of mind that brings into alignment your chatter and the body when executing a task. You're going to hear more about optimal performance. Seek to understand what this means by researching it more.

Simply put, enough adrenaline and other stress hormones in the body for the task. It's complicated how it all works and what goes on inside of you. The key to understanding optimal performance is recognizing that the current chatter in the present window is sending stress hormones into your body. You can have too much or not enough for the task and it all begins with your chatter.

Think of it this way. When you perform a task such as weight lifting or any task associated with competitive play, what are you thinking about? When you perform the task exceptionally well, your body is in an optimal state. The mind is focused, chatter is regulated and the emotional brain states are releasing the right amount of stress hormones for the task. This is what we refer to as an "optimal state". By your own personal design and self-discipline in your chatter, you have the right mixture of stress hormones to create the physical power to execute the task.

Your development goal is to learn this optimal state and call it up on demand at will. In your new journey of awareness and regulating the chatter, you will begin to take inventory on good thoughts and bad thoughts, good feelings and bad feelings. This "good" and "bad" is defined by how your body responds when supporting in a task. The good thoughts that motivate you and enable you to perform at peak with the right amount of stress hormones in your system are what we are seeking in your personal development.

If the unregulated negative chatter continues, fear, doubt and worry become the dominant emotional response. This in turn creates a state of frazzle or *"performance anxiety"*. Your unregulated chatter will constantly set off the emotional alarm releasing too much or too little stress hormones. This is bad business for many reasons. These stress hormones, which are intended to serve you, become a corrosive, toxic bath from being released too much and too often as a result of the negative chatter. It's called a state of frazzle and the extreme of which we have already learned is called an emotional highjack.

Chapter 6

Discovering the Chatter

"Thinking is nothing more than words and mental

pictures"

Self-talk is a common term often used to describe the chatter in your head. For the sake of instruction, self-talk and the chatter are referring to the same thing. The clinical term is "psycho-linguistic", psycho meaning the mind and linguistics meaning language. The critical lesson moving forward is that self-talk is nothing more than words and mental pictures randomly flashing in your mind at an extraordinarily fast pace.

These words and mental pictures constantly repeat and flash all day long without any effort from you. More importantly, some of these words and mental pictures are just plain trash and do not need to be in your head. You cannot prevent the negative chatter from popping up but you must take responsibility for it and learn to regulate or change it. Hold yourself accountable to the words and mental pictures because no one else can do it for you.

6.1.1 Guiding Principle: Fighting the Chatter

As a young athlete in the mid 1980's I struggled with negative chatter. Back then, if you told anyone that you have a voice in your head, they were going to put a white jacket on you and take you away. You didn't talk about it. The best answer I was ever given when talking about the chatter was simply, "don't talk back."

Literally, there was a time in my life when all I could do was try to shut down that negative chatter in my head. Just "turn it off" I would say to anyone willing to listen.

In 1988, I had just graduated from Purdue University. No job, no ideas and lots of un-answered questions. Life was complicated. I had a lot of questions and no clear answers. The negative thoughts seemed to beat me down until I became less and less motivated to even try. I later learned this sense of not knowing is a part of the set up in life, a season when nothing makes any sense.

It was time to take responsibility for my life, my career, and myself yet I didn't have a clue what was next. My internal dialogue seemed so loud, so frequent and so depressing. This was the first time in my life that I actually became of aware of the chatter and wanted so badly to turn it off.

By the grace of God, I found my way and in a few short years I had opened my first business, it was 1993. It took me over ten years to seek, study and learn more about self-talk so that I could begin understanding the value and the impact of the chatter. Now keep in mind, we didn't have today's knowledge or technology and most conversations about the chatter were minimized and at best you were told to keep it to yourself.

It was now 1998 and my business model started changing and focusing more on training and development. I began teaching and developing my own training material for corporate clients, the government and pretty much any one that wanted to listen and learn about becoming something more. As I matured and started to better understand the chatter, my desires to teach others about what goes on in the mind also started to grow.

It was during a leadership training session I was conducting with a group of critical care paramedics, when one paramedic in the front row raised his hand and asked, "How do you turn it off, the chatter in your head. How do you turn it off?"

"The chatter in your head is constant; there is no off switch"

I had to tell him the same truth that you must come to learn and accept. You can't. You cannot turn off the chatter. In the same way the heart beats, the lungs breath, the chatter chats. These physical features are designed for a purpose, but perhaps only one, the chatter, requires a disciplined approach. The chatter in your head is there for a reason and it can become your greatest asset if you learn how to regulate it. In the same respect, it can become your worst enemy if you pay no attention at all.

6.2.1 Reflection Exercise #1

In a moment, I want you to stop reading and try this exercise, one you should learn to practice often. Reflect back to a great performance you've had in the past, a time when you even surprised yourself. Who was watching? Who do you see standing around? What were you doing, what were you thinking? What were you feeling? You should write your responses down on paper. Your story should look something like this...

6.3.1 My Best Game

During my senior year of high school, in 1984, our team had advanced to the Semi-State Baseball Finals. Right before the big game, my father said to me, "Son, when you are standing there on deck, just see the ball hitting the bat." It sounded simple, no big deal. No one had ever mentioned the idea before and it didn't sound all that hard. In your imagination, simply visualize the ball hitting the bat. In other words, don't think about all the folks watching you or about the pressure to produce for your team, your coach. Don't worry about all the baseball scouts in the stands or about striking out or embarrassing yourself. Concentrate on one thing, the ball hitting the bat.

It was my best game ever. Three out of four at the plate; rocked the all-star pitcher that everyone came to see. One particular play comes to mind, a line drive triple to left center. It's so clear in my mind, even though it was over 30 years ago. I recall rounding second base in full stride, seeing my third base coach wave me on. As I slid into third base and popped up from the slide, I can see the wave of people standing and cheering. My coach jumping up and down, reaching for the sky and clapping with joy. In the midst of it all, in the cluster of fans, were my mother and father, jumping and screaming, celebrating the moment. I cherish these words and mental pictures we call memories, wonderful thoughts and emotions that seem like only yesterday. You, too must discipline your thoughts to find these memories and understand the power of positive thinking.

What a great, great game for me. Unfortunately, I was never able to duplicate it. I never understood the chatter well enough to make sense out of it. Although I continued to play the game, I could not deliver consistent results and my athletic career ended shortly afterwards.

Fleeting success is not the case for you. Fleeting means you achieve successful results, yet fail to be consistent in your efforts. Now we know the biggest culprit of poor performance is caused by anxiety, an emotional state created in the brain by negative self-talk. The chatter wasn't right for me but it can be right for you. You will learn these skills and the ability to summon your talent on demand by regulating your thoughts. This is your development goal. It starts now and you will practice daily.

Now, back to your exercise. We all have these special memories. Take the time to reflect back and tell me one of your stories. I want you to actually write it down and then send it to me from the website, www.ParrishTaylor.com. Be sure to "ink-it and not just think-it". Be clear in your vivid detail of what's happening inside and outside as best you can remember. Develop the skills to put words and mental pictures together and tell me your story. Write in your journal and reflect back with the greatest of detail these special moments in time. Use your words and memories to journey back; see the good and cherish the emotional response.

Trust me in faith on this exercise. It maybe difficult at first, but if you practice this reflection exercise and do it properly, it will become natural to you. This is a good habit of thinking and reflecting. Practice and it will become easier, even natural over time. You will understand later how this reflection on achievement will aid in your mental and emotional skill development.

Chapter 7

Mental Skill #3:

Organization

Definition: *"The ability to <u>inventory</u>; the <u>act</u> of creating a <u>detailed</u> <u>mental</u> <u>menu</u> <u>list</u> of words and mental pictures"*

We are talking about a mental skill and ability that can be learned over time with self-discipline and hard work. In the same way hard work and a strong work ethic will reap rewards with physical strength training and conditioning, the same is true with mental strength and conditioning.

The hard work of mental and emotional strength training reap the reward of handling pressure and difficult situations, overcoming conflicts and problem solving. The rewards actually result in improved decision-making and your ability to keep cool and calm. Your decision-making will improve under pressure and during difficult situations.

This is a critical stepping-stone in your development process. Once you've become aware of the chatter, you begin to regulate it; the scriptures call this "taking your thoughts captive". In flexing the mental skill of organization, you learn to file the chatter away for inventory later; some chatter you want to get rid of entirely. You learn to organize your thoughts. Remember, as soon as you file one set of words and mental pictures, more thoughts will rapidly follow. It's a constant cycle.

You already know thoughts arrive in rapid time. The key step now is to understand your role in navigating this tidal wave of words and mental pictures. You must discipline the important thoughts by making a detailed mental list. Of course, you are encouraged to "ink it, not just think it". The act of writing things down is not always necessary for every task but there will be times of intense pressure that writing on paper will "free up the mind". Think of your computer system and the need to add more RAM (or random access memory). The moment you write your thoughts down on paper it's like adding computer RAM and giving yourself more thinking power to focus.

In this case, understand your brain is so powerful you can create "filing cabinets" to creatively store your thoughts for later. As each thought pops up, you must learn to put some of those words and mental pictures on the shelf and deal with them later, not now. A good guiding principle to use when organizing your thoughts is to consider only 20% are worthy to keep in your chatter. Most everything else must be stored away and inventoried for later.

Mental: "Learning to regulate the chatter" 85

At this stage of your mental skill development the third mental skill will continue to improve your ability in awareness and regulation of your emotional states. You must first learn and understand the mental skills of regulating the chatter before you are able to engage your mental skill sets to regulate your emotions.

Earlier in the book we used a creative example of "two-brains" and how they relate to one another. We talked about having a thinking brain and a feeling brain. In this example we learned the feeling brain can highjack the thinking brain. The feeling brain takes over and just like turning up the volume knob on your radio, the feeling brain turns up the volume of stress hormones in your body.

The brain's emotional states regulate the amount of adrenaline and other stress hormones that are released into your system and it all starts with your ability to regulate the chatter. When you learn to inventory the right and specific words and mental pictures that support you, you then can regulate the volume knob on the feeling brain. When the feeling brain turns up just enough volume for the right amount of stress hormones for the task science calls this "flow". The opposite of "flow" we've already referenced as "frazzle". If "flow" is the right amount of stress hormones for the task and "frazzle" is a fragmented, too much or too little amount of stress hormones for the task, it is your mental skill and ability to navigate between the two. In sports language, this state of "flow" is often referred to as "the zone".

7.1.1 Guiding Principle: Recovery is key

This is not about prevention, but rather recovery. "Frazzle" and an emotional highjack is a part of life, we must all learn to accept this truth. This is not about controlling or preventing negative thoughts from popping up or having negative feelings about yourself or others. It is impossible to control your thoughts and emotions, never use the word "control" when it comes to these two subjects. These are involuntary body functions; your focus is to develop the skills to recover from these internal states.

Learn to seek understanding on why we all have these negative thoughts and emotional overloads. It is your goal to accept and no longer struggle with why or how often these negative thoughts and emotions appear; it is simply the way you are designed. When you consider these first three mental skills, we can begin to explain your new knowledge like this…

> *"Your communication to yourself (self-talk) and your ability to concentration, repeating often with focus strengthens your ability to organization complimentary words and store them in your mental menu list, these three skills and ability will empower you to recover from negative chatter and emotional frazzle".*

If you really drill down into the science of frazzle and emotional highjack, you will be amazed at what happens inside of you when the chatter is running rampant, unregulated and unorganized. As you journey through life and compete, you will wig yourself out with negative chatter from time to time; it will happen. Struggle not! How frequently and how often you recover is determined by your ability to flex these mental skills.

7.2 Natural Law: The Law of Correspondence

This is another natural law like the Law of Gravity and the Law of Concentration mentioned earlier. The Law of Correspondence says, *"Your outer world is a reflection of your inner world".* Simply put, your chatter on the inside will determine what you see on the outside.

Remember, this is a natural law, so nature is the judge. You can't plead not-guilty or even ignorance and expect to get a break on this law or reap the benefits. You will either reap the benefits and rewards, or you will suffer the consequences. The kicker is only you will ever know your truth. Only you know what's happening inside your chatter. Since this is your chatter and it's inside of you, you then are responsible for obeying this nature law; only you can hold yourself accountable to the benefits or consequences.

"Only you know the dominant thoughts in your head"

A great illustration of the suffering and consequence of this law is when everyone on the outside applauds you, yet you allow your chatter inside to remain self-critical. You not only miss the sincere nourishing words of a compliment, instead, you override it with your own toxic chatter. Ironically, your lack of skill and ability to accept a compliment is a critical indicator of your low self-esteem and how you truly feel about yourself. If you cannot learn to accept a sincere compliment and say, thank you it is painfully obvious you are suffering from unregulated chatter. Unregulated chatter, which is working against your ability to grow, to achieve, and become something more than you are right now.

"Your voice inside is louder than anyone on the outside; your voice will over-ride all the others."

7.3.1 Guiding Principle: Performance Improvement

All performance improvement begins with new words and mental pictures on how you want things to happen. This is the most critical "mental menu list" of all.

The inner world comes first. You must take the time

to define what is important to you, your dreams, your goals and desires, the results that you specifically want in life and in competition. It's ok to borrow from your coach or your boss, but you must still have the discipline to create your "mental list" of words and mental pictures which support you. You must define and refine often and then store in your inventory. They are what you refer back to as you learn to flex your mental skill of organization and file away all the bad images. It's this "mental list" of values you create that will become the filtering system on what's good and needs to stay in the chatter and what's filtered out as "discontinued" and should be taken out as trash to the curb.

The lack of a "mental list" of values can be considered the consequence of rambling chatter. This rambling, unorganized chatter ultimately affects your decision making in the moment. You will lack discernment and the ability to judge what is right and wrong in that moment.

7.3.2 Guiding Principle: Disciplined Chatter

"We must all suffer one of two pains, the pain of

discipline or the pain of regret. Do not trade one for the other; discipline weighs ounces where as regret weighs tons." – Jim Rohn

Keep in mind these skills require work. There is a self-discipline that must be applied to your chatter; the five skills simply provide you with a framework to get started. You must work hard at finding these skills in your daily life and develop them. It is the same for anything worthy of achievement. If you do not work, you will not reap the benefits, but rather suffer the consequences of a rambling, unregulated chatter that ultimately seals your fate. Your soul will die young and we will bury you somewhere down the long road of a miserable life.

Understand that anything of value requires work; it is not free. These benefits and ideas are available to you and within your reach. However, there is no entitlement, you will not benefit from this skills without hard work and self-discipline.

Most people around you are comfortable with just trying to get through life or playing an average game.

We call it "mediocrity", where you simply settle and the quality of your game suffers. Rather than working on the chatter and developing these mental skills, to often, we turn on the radio, pull up the new app, and switch on the TV or the computer. We seek entertainment or anything to keep us from hanging out with "self" and trying to better understand the chatter. I've been there. It was only later in life when I learned these valuable truths that I can share here and now, long after my time for playing competitive sports and competing in athletic competition has ended.

Whatever chatter you allow inside, true or false, organized or unorganized, influences your view to the outside. If the dominant message in your chatter is "poor student and struggling", 'choke and can't', or even 'unworthy and don't belong', odds are your emotional state will trigger feelings of doubt, confusion, fear, even anxiety, and your report card will confirm your doubt. The same is true with your personal view and your inner dialogue regarding your ability to compete at an elite and world-class level of play.

You must learn to turn off the distractions and place inventory on your chatter; learn to have quality conversations with yourself. You learn to regulate the chatter and talk with yourself on the important things. It is the world according to you. It's your world; you must make it happen and organize the inside to realize it on the outside.

Make It Happen
"I believe in the power of these words so much, they are inked on my flesh."

It was 1989 and I was twenty-one years old. My athletic identity was no longer and the college-student lifestyle was over. In reflection it took me about three years on my own before I realized I was going nowhere. My chatter made me feel lost in life and no clear direction of what to do next. I was twenty-five at the time.

I struggled a few more years and in 1992 something changed for me; I started regulating the chatter. It was a slow process, at least for me. At that point I had twenty-five years of trashy, uncertain and unregulated chatter and I had poorly programmed myself.

This was a time that I call the, "awakening". It was the first time in my life that I started paying more attention to the inside than the outside. The search inside began and I started to learn more and more about who I was and what strengths and talents I had been given. I was able to use the ideas and tools mentioned in this book to learn more about my weaknesses and how to improve. And it was then I learned how to take my talents and serve others.

This is a time to turn off the TV and radio. Put all the devices down and learn how to hang out with yourself, learn how to have good conversations about who you are and your true potential.

7.3.3 Guiding Principle: The Mind is like a Missal

Technology today allows our most advance military strikes to achieve their objectives with great accuracy from miles and miles away. Your mind works much in the same way with its own "on-board navigational system." This is another one of those amazing abilities and roles that your brain plays in your ability to hit your own targets.

For the missile, it takes a very specific set of "x" and "y" coordinates to strike the target. For you to achieve, grow and become more skilled and competitive it also takes a very specific set of "x" and "y" coordinates. In order to strike your targets and achieve daily goals requires a constant, organized set of words and mental pictures. In other words, your words and mental pictures are the specific set of coordinates. You will be amazed with how well you will perform a task once you align the chatter with the specific coordinates required for your achievement.

7.3.4 Guiding Principle: First Words

The Olympian athletes are taught to focus on and repeat power words. It's an exercise using the five mental skills that allow you to work your brain states and your chatter to your advantage. You're going to have chatter anyway, but if you discipline your chatter and create a library of one-word adjectives that create the right emotional states to perform your task, you will improve your level of play.

For example, if the task is hitting or catching the ball or making a critical kick, your "first words" might be, "Power". "Strength". "Focus". "Sight". "Stride". These are your chatter-coordinates. Notice, there is not a lot of chatter going on by design. You are focused on specific words and mental pictures and constantly feeding your brain with this first words in your chatter. These power words should emphasize your ability to perform the task exceptionally well. Even though you physically will not perform the task until later in the afternoon or tomorrow. This is what we call "pre-playing" in the future-window. You are learning to summon your talent on demand and in the moment the more you learn to "pre-play" specific chatter for upcoming events. These first-words that you have learned to define for every task will in turn support your need for the brain's specific set of "x" and "y" coordinates.

Chapter 8

Alonzo Goes To

Nebraska

"These five mental skills are transferable; the same five will help you achieve in all domains, in life and in competition"

On July 27th, 2011, we were sitting in the Lincoln Nebraska airport returning home after a visit with the Nebraska Football Coaches. I almost missed something so subtle. These five mental skills are transferable.

The three of us sat in the airport. Dr. Garrison, Alonzo's mentor, was on the computer while Alonzo was on a phone interview with Rivals.com. As the two sat watching the Rivals website changed word for word during Alonzo's interview, I reflected back pulling up my own words and mental pictures of Alonzo talking with different coaches.

During the two full days of meeting with coaches and taking the tours, Nebraska demonstrated how much they wanted Alonzo. From the moment we stepped onto the campus, the "wow" factor was everywhere.

One individual conversation kept popping up in my brain. Our final meeting of the day was with Tim Beck, Nebraska's quarterback coach. It was this conversation with Coach Beck I was able to re-affirm for Alonzo how his five mental skills were working during the meeting. At this point, we needed Alonzo

Mental: "Learning to regulate the chatter"

to better understand how to apply the five mental skills in the classroom. At the time, Alonzo's GPA did not meet the minimum required by the National Collegiate Athlete Association (NCAA).

Coach Beck greeted us with a smile and came right to the point by saying, "Others have talked to you about what we can do here at Nebraska. I want to show you". Immediately he pulled up a long list of game films and before we even sat down, Coach Beck had us all staring at the big-screen, watching Nebraska game plays.

The dialogue between Coach Beck and Alonzo was amazing. Watching them review Nebraska plays and respond to defensive players created so much energy in the room. Even the coaches sitting around the perimeter of the room were on the edge of their seats. Coach Beck would start the game film, stop suddenly, and fire a question at Alonzo. In a calm, cool manner, Alonzo would give a specific, detailed, yet short answer. Alonzo was in the zone, "flow" was the emotional state and judging from the coaches in the room, Alonzo nailed it every single time.

On the outside, there was every reason to be overwhelmed, "frazzle" and an emotional state of highjack. The visit to the Nebraska campus and football stadium, the hospitality from all the coaches and staff, the magnificent facility, the friendly people and players, the heritage and legacy in the Nebraska football program. We actually sat in Tom Osborne's office; the man is a legend. And yet Alonzo was able to regulate his thoughts and emotions with no signs of distress, fear or anxiety.

On the inside, at least for Alonzo, he concentrated and was organized. He knew his priorities and was prepared for every question and provided the correct answer within a mere 3-5 seconds. Alonzo was at peace. He was in the "optimal state" of "flow"; he was clearly in the "zone".

He was feeling his motivation for the game. He was in the moment. The rush of adrenalin from thinking about what to do, 'go left or go right, go high or go low'. He was in the now, in the moment of each step of the play as it unfolded on the big-screen.

Mental: "Learning to regulate the chatter"

Regardless of what was going on around him, Alonzo had the presence of mind in the moment, delivering the right amount of stress hormones and adrenaline for the task. For well over forty-five minutes, Coach Beck challenged Alonzo with questions and seemed intrigued with every response.

So there we are, back at the Lincoln airport, replaying my own game film from an hour earlier watching Alonzo and Coach Beck. At this point, I am past all the glamour and glitter of the visit and focused on the problem. Why the academic struggle?

If these five mental skills are truly transferable, why is there optimal performance on the athletic field of play and poor sub-standard performance in the classroom?

It's obvious that Alonzo can summon his talents and flex his mental skills on demand. Athletically, in most cases, achieve extraordinary results. We can clearly show how Alonzo uses his five mental skills on the field in competition and as a result, his physical ability stands out and amazes everyone. And yet,

Mental: "Learning to regulate the chatter"   102

academically, there is a struggle to achieve the necessary results.

And that's when it hit me. Alonzo was suffering from poor conditioning and a lack of academic motivation.

If my theories were correct, we could break through the academic hurdles and at the same time, strengthen his athletic performance. Once we learn awareness to these mental skills, we can transfer these skill sets and ultimately improve decision-making in all aspects of life.

8.1 Conditioning & Motivation:

As we stood there in the airport, I called Alonzo over to an empty ticket counter where we could talk. It was time for a development plan to start re-conditioning his belief system and the tool to use was his internal chatter.

At best, Alonzo had been a below average student his entire academic life. His unregulated chatter for over sixteen years would repeat these false accusations and over time Alonzo, like you and I, we start to believe these lies. He would hear it at home, he would hear it at school from his teachers and guidance counselors and without fail his daily assignments and report card would validate this lie that he was and always will be a weak student.

As we stood there at that empty ticket counter, I wrote down the following words on piece of paper, *"I am a good learner"*. I asked Alonzo to write these words in his notebook and repeat them for me ten times out loud. He played along, although you could see his doubt and confusion.

I asked Alonzo, *"Do you believe that? Do you believe you are a good learner?"* He paused for a moment, as if searching for the correct answer rather than the truth. He gave me the "yes" but I could hear and see the hesitation. He didn't really believe it.

Together, we reflected back and talked about the time with Coach Beck. He agreed it was a magical moment and after a little coaching, he could see the mental skills at work during the time and talks with Coach Beck.

Mental: "Learning to regulate the chatter" 104

This was the affirmation Alonzo needed, in order to see it for himself. He now had proof that in mere seconds, he could read the defensive players and make quick decisions on what action to take next. His natural motivation for the game made learning the defense easy and his ability to learn and respond came natural and quick.

Alonzo was an exceptional learner and now he had the proof to validate this idea in his chatter. Alonzo couldn't deny his ability to learn the defense and respond with the correct answer when talking with Coach Beck. Motivated by the game, watching game films (mental images), flexing his mental muscle (five skills), Alonzo had impressed the entire room. He demonstrated his ability to learn the defense quickly and respond on demand and in the moment.

The working theory was to coach Alonzo on how to discipline his chatter with *"I am a good learner"*.

This statement is a great example of a simple, short series of first-words that supported his task. He had enough evidence to believe the statement was true. It was up to him to discipline his mind and repeat it often in order to build and re-condition his belief system for academic success.

The next challenge was motivation. How to motivate Alonzo with academic achievement in the same way he was motivated by playing the game of football?

I ask Alonzo if there were any highlights from the last couple of days, anything that really impressed him or felt special. As he began to speak, I could see the opportunity and told him to take a moment to write a few things down. He was encouraged to "ink it and not just think" so we could review and discuss later.

He listed all seven coaches that he spoke with and highlights from each conversation. What caught my eye were the references he made about school. He wrote, "*I like how they are interested in my studies. How dedicated they are to the players in the classroom. The entire team earned a 3.0 GPA.*"

This was the missing motivational-link we needed for Alonzo, a personal experience to nourish his much-need academic self-motivation. It was on this piece of paper we were able to find his new words and mental pictures to motivate achievement in the classroom. The Nebraska experience of walking through the study lounge, meeting his personal study "mentor" and the structured approach of combining athletics and academics made a critical impression on Alonzo. In other words, these seven coaches and the new conversations about how important his grades were and more importantly all the resources that would be made available to him to ensure his success motivated him to new academic achievement.

Alonzo's chatter was seeking inward and looking at what he liked and what motivated him from the two-day experience. All the talk and attention on grades and study support would aide in his self-motivation to achieve more in the classroom. After speaking about the experience with Coach Beck, Alonzo recognized his ability to learn and now had the right motivation to apply his mental skills in the classroom.

The notes that follow are actual remarks and assignments from that day and weeks to come when working with Alonzo. I've included these remarks in the book as more insights and examples on how we can all take these complicated subjects and learn to break down the ideas and disciplines and begin putting them to use in your day to day chatter.

8.2 Working Notes:

Self-Reliant (reference the Emotional Intelligence profile); Alonzo had scored low on this critically important competency of emotional intelligence. This profiling tool would enable us to bridge the gap between applying his five mental skills and daily achievement. It was important that Alonzo learned to rely more on his own inner dialogue rather than the opinions and views of others around him. The solution was awareness and disciplined chatter on his daily achievements. He was instructed to reflect back in the past-window at the end of each day and talk to himself about what he accomplished on his own.

8.2.1 Assignment #1

(Conditioning & Re-Programming)

"I am a good learner". Alonzo was encouraged to say it often and confirm it with repetition in his inner dialogue. He was instructed to write this phase fifty times daily and then supporting it with little achievements from the day such as learning a new football play, working to learn a new subject from class.

8.2.2 Assignment #2 (Self Reliance)

Daily Achievement: Using another tool that we teach within the mental and emotional training program, Alonzo was encouraged to use his "Six-cylinder" list and identify in writing at least ten small daily goals he wanted to achieve. For example, the easy goals like praying, attending football practice, going to each class. He was encouraged to find the easy, low hanging fruit in order to discipline him for achievement of the larger more complex goals.

At the end of each day, reflect back through the past-window and hold himself accountable to achieving his goals. The objective here is to reflect at the end of each day and seek out your achievements. It's more than simply checking things off the to-do list. It's to discipline yourself and look back at your little achievements that will in turn prepare you for even

Mental: "Learning to regulate the chatter"

greater achievements down the road. You must learn to nourish this achievement drive within yourself by reflecting back correctly each and every day.

Chapter 9

Mental Skill #4:

Discrimination

Definition: "The ability to <u>prioritize</u> the words and the mental pictures"

You understand thoughts come rapid; the chatter is often fast and furious. For those in my generation, you might remember the first screen-saver on your old computer called "star-field". It was basically a dark space background with hundreds of white-dots that looked like little stars coming at you. Whether you set the speed for fast or slow, there were still a million stars coming off the screen at you, so similar to the thousands of thoughts with each passing moment.

You must learn how to prioritize your chatter. Discrimination means the ability to rank your chatter as it's coming at you. For example, if you are sitting in a boring class or meeting you know that your mind will begin to wander off. You must decide what is most important in that moment and prioritize your thoughts. You must continue to prioritize which words and mental pictures are the most important and you must learn to do this all the time. It is a constant and continual skill you have to exercise, knowing there is competition between good chatter and bad chatter. In other words, bad chatter is a constant threat, and good chatter must always be on guard and only you can do it.

Determining which words are important enough to occupy your chatter is the critical mental skill of discrimination. It's your choice to prioritize your words and mental pictures, given the desires and goals you wish to achieve. Get it done and prepare to be challenged. If you fail, your chatter will waste more and more of your time of each day. You need to know and understand how to build and achieve your goals daily by prioritizing your chatter.

A wise man once said, "the penny watches the dollar". In other words, the little daily achievements add up to the larger achievements down the road. The little daily chats in your self-talk are the pennies that add up to the almighty dollar of achievement. This is a critical life lesson that applies to your personal daily agenda 86,400 seconds of every day.

9.1.1 Guiding Principle: Who's responsible?

It is your chatter; you are responsible for the language in your mind. Only you can hold yourself accountable to what's actually going on inside.

The only thing we know is what you say. If I were to

ask you *"what's on your mind",* you can lie and no one would ever know, including you if you're not careful. Only you are going to know what chatter you allow and whether it's helping or hurting you. Only you know if you're thinking about the right words and right mental pictures.

The mental skill of discrimination must be engaged, regardless of which window you find yourself thinking. Your chatterbox is running right now, as always. The "now" is so critical in building your awareness.

In the now, the present-window, you will find your thoughts flashing words and mental pictures replaying events from the past or pre-playing upcoming events from the future-window. You must reflect back with discipline, and prioritize which words and mental pictures you will allow. In the same respect, you must pre-play with discipline and prioritize which words and mental pictures support your performance.

The mental skill of discrimination is your ability to prioritize the chatter. Regardless of which window you are thinking the negative toxic thoughts will appear and it's your ability to engage this skill that keeps you on track for future achievement. Remember, the mind can only hold one thought at a time. It is very important you regulate and prioritize which you allow to dominate.

9.1.2 Guiding Principle: Window of the future

This is very important as it pertains to your next opportunity to demonstrate your physical ability. You must learn to always win and see yourself achieving in the present and future-window.

There is another note worthy scene in Kevin Costner's movie, "For the Love of the Game." When it comes to discrimination, sometimes you're going to have people in your world who say and do things that will work against your achievement. They simply will not see your ability to grow and achieve. Truth be told, they may be a distraction in your chatter and their words will keep popping up. They're going to talk and use words that if you're not careful, will get into your head and hold you back.

In this classic scene, Costner's character is injured and he is working to recover so he can play one last career game. Costner is speaking with his trainer in a casual conversation when all of a sudden; the trainer slips up and not even paying attention, says, *"If you make it back…"*

Costner's response is the exact tone and discipline you must carry when surrounding yourself with others. The final words of this scene, as Costner storms out of the room, *"You said if, you said if I make it back. You either get your mind right and help me recover or don't comeback here. I'll do my job, you do yours!"*

You are going to have people close to you, who are going to offer opinions and half-hearted effort and the fact is they may hold you back unintentionally. They will use words and offer opinions which will contaminate your thinking, but only if you allow it. Understand this concept; see those around you and learn to filter their words rather than struggle with conflicting opinions. When you develop your mental skills for achievement, you indirectly prepare yourself for the outside chatter and learn to prioritize it.

"Let no one's opinion of you become your reality"

Let me say it again. I want you to write it down. *Let no one's opinion of you become your reality.* Let no one's opinion, be it words or mental pictures, penetrate your chatter where it becomes the dominant message. Don't do it. Do not allow it to happen. If you are done, be done because you are ready and not because someone else said you are not good enough.

9.1.3 Guiding Principle: "80/20" Rule

The "80/20" rule applies to everything. If you want to become a better competitor, the "80/20" rule applies. If you want to become a better weightlifter, the "80/20" rule applies. If you want to be a better coach, a better father, a better son or daughter, a better spouse, the role does not matter. If you want more, apply the "80/20" rule to everything.

The best way to understand the "80/20" rule is in the form of a question. What are the few things (20%) that make the biggest difference (80%)?

One critical question you must learn to seek out in the chatter is what are the few things or the 20%. Given

Mental: "Learning to regulate the chatter"   117

your past, given your poor programming, your handicaps, and everything else outside and in, what words and mental pictures do you need in the chatter that will make the biggest difference?

This is about your mental skill and ability to discriminate, prioritize the words and mental pictures in your chatter. The ability to regulate the self-talk and say, *"that's not important right now. Here's what I need in my chatter, these are the few things I need in my chatter right here, right now."*

It is not a good priority to start beating yourself up after a task. It's natural, yes, but beating yourself up will not qualify as one of the few things making a big difference in your success. You must learn to change the way you react to certain situations and poor performance. It's a constant thing and you must learn awareness.

In our leadership class, we teach what is called a "task analysis". This helps bring structure to your chatter. When you find your self-talk wandering and working against you, having the little dominos from your task analysis helps you to regulate and prioritize. Without the task list, you may continue to struggle in the chatter and never get past awareness. Awareness, by comparison, is simple. It is regulating that requires stronger and conditioned mental skills.

When you conduct your own task analysis, regardless of the task, you are breaking down all the little dominos or actions you must take to achieve and execute the task successfully (or in some cases, exceptionally well). As you define all the actions, by refining the task list, you will determine little sub-groups or sub-tasks that sometimes get hidden and are ultimately what's holding you back. This refined list of sub-tasks will become your specific and prioritized words and mental pictures that help you grow and achieve the next level of performance. Learn to ask yourself often, *"What is important to me? Given my desires and goals to achieve more what words and mental pictures support the vision?"* This is how you put your mental skill of discrimination to work in your 86,400 seconds of the day so that your mental recorder captures and conditions for future performance.

Chapter 10

Mental Skill #5:

Innovation

Definition: *"The ability to <u>create</u> <u>new</u> words and <u>new</u>*
mental pictures in the moment"

You have five mental skills that can be described as abilities. You are able to communicate with yourself and select specific words and you are able to do this on demand.

You are able to focus or concentrate by repeating specific words over time and you are able to do this for an extended period of time on demand.

You are able to inventory and create a personal list of words that help you with decision-making and you are able to access this list on demand.

You are able to prioritize and discriminate different words, some should be repeated often and some should not be allowed and you are able to do this on demand.

The fifth and final mental skill is known as innovation. This is the ability to be creative and thinking of new words and new mental pictures and this ability is a skill demonstrated when you create these new words on demand.

There are going to be times when you find yourself under attack in the chatter. You will find yourself weak and the dominant words are, "its not possible". You will struggle to see yourself winning or achieving in your mind and your words will work against you.

These are the times when courage and faith come into maturity; optimism becomes the dominant thought when you learn to develop this mental skill. You must learn how to see it for yourself. You must discipline very specific words and very specific mental pictures that see you executing the necessary tasks to achieve the next step. Truth told, until you mature into this enlightened self-interest your personal achievement and ability to problem solve and overcome conflict will be limited. The collateral damage from your lack of personal skill development will then flow over into your relationships when you fail to connect with others. As a result your relationships suffer and so too will the team unit or family.

Remember back to the illustration of the two brains, the thinking brain and the feeling brain. Once the feeling brain begins to highjack the thinking brain, creativity and your ability to innovate is hindered, even limited. If you think you have control or can prevent this from happening, you cannot. You cannot prevent the brain from playing this role of a highjack. Yours is to develop the ability to become aware when it's happening inside of you and then learn to regulate the highjack by bringing the thinking brain back on line with specific words and mental pictures (recovery).

For most of us it is difficult to be creative when under pressure. When you are in an unregulated emotional state of frazzle, your ability to learn is hindered. The brain functions you need the most to make wise decisions for the task at hand are the least accessible. Once you begin to understand and accept this critical truth to how the body responds to pressure we can now better understand why the mental and emotional preparation is so critical. We must learn to be aware of the little penny-conversations we have with ourselves throughout the day. When we learn this 86-4 level of awareness and regulate the chatter, we in turn begin to program (in some cases re-program) past, present and future events.

10.1.1 Guiding Principle: Innovate

When you innovate, you are using your creative brainpower. Your creativity is often hindered when you are under pressure, dealing with stress or the extreme, distressed. As you journey through your day it's possible to have many low-grade highjacks that begin to add up and before you realize it your stress hormone levels are through the roof and you haven't even left the house yet.

You wake up late from the lack of sleep (low-grade highjack and lack of physical rest), you spill your coffee on your outfit and no time to change (another low-grade shot of stress hormones into the system) and your chatter runs rampant with words on being late for your first meeting and you are soon sitting on the side of the road talking with the police officer. All of these minor events and lack of regulating the chatter will eventually add up to the point where you and your performance are hindered.

In order to work on a corrective action to improve your performance, you are required to recover from the highjack. Once you recover, you can then begin to seek and discover what adjustments in your task execution need to be made and/or prepared for and refined in the menu list. It is your ability to recover that sets the foundation for your own ability to seek out new words and new mental pictures that get you back on track. The mental skill of innovation is a learned behavior that empowers you to begin the recovery process for developing and improving your next performance.

For the sake of learning, this is a very elementary view of what's happening inside of you as your chatter dictates to your body's stress response system. The next time you become aware that you are "wigging" yourself out simply begin to talk to yourself by asking specific questions. By engaging your brain with a question, blood flow increases back to the brain where you need it the most in this critical moment.

"When you ask yourself questions, it's like making the brain mad."

Understand what is happening in your body when you are energized and in competition. Your energy is based on your body's ability to increase blood flow. When you get a jolt of stress hormones, your lungs take in more oxygen while your heart will increase and pump more blood to the body. All of this happens inside of you to support your physical ability to perform the task.

The one thing you need the most under pressure is the least accessible during a highjack, the thinking brain. You must learn to recover and get the thinking brain back on line and to do so simply ask yourself questions targeting thoughts and emotions.

10.1.2 Guiding Principle: Two Questions

What am I thinking? What am I feeling?

These are two very specific "x" and "y" questions or coordinates that you have designed and placed on your mental menu list. These two simple questions are so good, we teach you to use these throughout the day. These two questions help you learn awareness to your thoughts (chatter) and feelings (emotions). Keep in mind, the goal is awareness 86,400 seconds of every day.

When you ask yourself these questions, blood flow goes back to the brain. In theory, your disciplined chatter makes the brain mad and this causes the blood to flow back to the thinking brain. This promotes recovery in order to get the thinking brain back on line with rational, wise decision-making. It is at this point you have a chance to recover from your emotional highjack and regain your ability to innovate, be creative and learn.

It is difficult. You must work through the process of regulating the chatter. You step out in faith, going beyond what your sensory perception tells you, and commit to it in your chatter. You will amaze yourself with what's possible for you and your un-tapped potential. You will no longer live with "impossibility-thinking" but rather self-discipline the brains optimal states by what is called "possibility-thinking".

"You must learn to see it for yourself before others will see it in you"

In other words, you just had a bad performance. You are growing and becoming something more by working on your mental skills. Your mental skills are the one thing you can actually put forth a small amount of work and reap amazing rewards and many times the rewards of mental discipline are immediate.

10.1.3 Guiding Principle: Performance Improvement

You will find your thoughts rewinding and reflecting back, your chatter is looking through the past-window. Be aware to catch the negative words and mental pictures that pop up in your mind. Your goal will be to pull from your mental menu list these two questions that are designed as "x" and "y" coordinates, each supporting a "performance improvement" strategy. This strategy is designed to support the way your brain functions during problem solving and conflict resolution.

For example, you are not performing well and your stats are confirming this reality. You have a potential problem and you are now seeking a new solution based on your internal dialogue. The new, innovative solution is to use these mental skills before, during and after you are working on your physical skills and fundamentals to the game you play. Yes, you must continue to put in the hours of physical practice and drill instruction. However, now you are also strengthening your mental and emotional skills at the same time you are practicing the physical skills. This improvement strategy basically keeps your chatter focused on achievement rather than setbacks.

Question #1: What did I do right?

This is your "Atta-boy". You must discipline your chatter to seek these answers out when you reflect back in the window of the past. Reflect back and learn to review your own personal motives when you were performing well. Seek out what was motivating you and take the necessary time to find the words and mental pictures that were flashing in your chatter while you were performing so well. Simply remember your mental recorder is capturing everything, and will serve you these "Atta-boys" later. It's amazing how God set this up to work inside of you and it is all based on your chatter in the present-window.

The question, "what did I do wrong" is the natural and the negative one we all ask from time to time. Struggle not! You must understand this is the natural rattle of an unorganized, unregulated chatter and it is so by design. The brain's role as a security guard for you and your bodies natural response to every situation is naturally going to seek out the threat and all that's wrong.

Question #2 (with self-discipline):
    What can I do better?

The kicker is that you have been given the mental recorder; the all powerful, all amazing mental recorder that will either serve you or beat you with the dominant message from your chatter.

By asking a short specific question seeking the "do-better", your chatter engages blood flow and seeks to innovate. Creativity uses the intellectual brain to make domino corrections; basically refining the "x" and "y" coordinates for the next time you do the task. Your mental recorder is paying attention and captures your answers to be pulled up for the next time. The short story is your brain's pre-programmed responses will support and engineer your performance in the future. All based on your chatter in the present-window.

"Your mental skills and ability will engage you to see yourself winning at every level of executing a task."

When my mentor first introduced these ideas about the skill of innovation he added this subtle little note:

"The skill of innovation is like striving to achieve greatness and to over come the highest mountain top; realizing you will never get there."

When you understand the foundation to this skill of innovation, the short story is that you will never be as good as you can be. You must continue to grow and become something more than you are today. This mental skill of innovation will continue to challenge you to tackle the next mountaintop regardless of where you are in your life achievements.

10.1.4 Guiding Principle: It's Possible

Two words when focused and repeated often with purpose and reason will change your belief system. It's possible.

Honestly, if someone else can do it, why not you? No this is not a warm fuzzy motivational speech it's a real question for you to take ownership in the chatter. Each one of us has everything to gain from seeking the truth in this "possibility-thinking".

Even today I am learning to accept this truth, it is possible for me, and it is possible for you. In my own efforts to practice, preach, and teach, I too must discipline the chatter at times and believe that its possible for me to become more. It is possible for me to become a better teacher, a better writer, a better dad, a better husband, and a better business partner. And yes, even you with all that you have achieved, all that you have become at this point in your life… it is still possible to become something more. Humbly and respectfully becoming something more to yourself and those around you.

There are going to be times when you don't have the answer. You don't have the mental pictures and the only two words you can muster up are going to be, *"it's possible"*.

Chapter 11

Stress verse Distress

"Stress is a natural part of the body and it's way to rise to the occasion for a task. The goal is not to get read of stress, the goal is to get the right kind of stress. When it's the right kind of stress, we love it."

"Distress: The Body's Silent Killer"

We are discussing the internal dialogue and how this directly affects your body's stress response. Remember the earlier illustration of two brains, a thinking brain and a feeling brain. We discovered when the chatter is unregulated its nature is to be toxic or negative. The negative chatter then creates the emotional highjack and the feeling brain hits the panic button, which releases adrenaline and other stress hormones into your system. This is natural by design and a wonderful illustration of the brain and body working together.

The brain sends the body a signal to the adrenal gland located in your mid-section. The release of these stress hormones enables your body to support you on the task and rise to the occasion in the moment. Your blood pressure goes up. Your blood flow to the limbs increases. Your breathing pattern varies and there are so many other physical signs that you will learn to monitor and regulate.

If the chatter is negative for an extended period of time, these stress hormones start to work against you. When this happens, an emotionally distressed state occurs in the body from an overload of these stress hormones. As a result, your decision-making is hindered and your ability to perform a routine task can be greatly altered even after thousands of hours of practice and repetition. In the National Geographic documentary, "Distress: Portrait of a killer", researchers say:

> *"To make sense of what's happening in your body, you've got these two hormones that are the workhorses of the whole stress response. One of them we all know, adrenaline, American version epinephrine. The other is a less known hormone called Glucocorticoids. It comes out of the adrenal gland along with adrenaline. These are the two backbones to the body's stress response system. The stress response and those two hormones are critical to our survival. When you run for your life (or basically the extreme of pressure) basics are all that matter. Lungs work overtime to pump mammoth quantities of oxygen into the bloodstream. The heart races to pump that oxygen throughout the body so muscles*

respond instantly. You need your blood pressure up to deliver that energy. You need to turn off anything that's not essential, growth, reproduction, you know, you're running for your life this is no time to ovulate, tissue repair, all that sort of thing. Do it later if there is a later".

Follow the sequence of events inside of you, all starting with your chatter. The thinking brain repeats the negative, the feeling brain hits the panic button and sends a signal down to your body's adrenal glands and you get a flood of stress hormones. Too many stress hormones for an extended period of time begin to work against you and your future performance. Too little stress hormones and you lack the necessary motivation and energy to act in excellence. You need to know this and what's happening in your body all based on what you allow in your thought patterns.

Your body responds to the stress hormones in different ways. You need to learn to detect subtle clues or signals. For example, you might feel a little sweat above the brow. Your breathing rate changes, you might take shorter breaths and your blood pressure will rise from your heart beating faster. You might have a tingle and need to use the bathroom. These are all signs you must learn to monitor that indicate a low (or high grade) emotional highjack. The research on stress and the body go on to say,

"When the animal escapes the pressure, its stress response shuts down, but human beings can't seem to find the off switch. We turn on the exact same stress response for purely psychological states thinking about the ozone layer, the taxes coming up, mortality, thirty-year mortgages, we turn on the same stress response and the key difference is we're not doing it for a real physiological reason and we're doing it non-stop. By not turning off the stress response when reacting to life's traffic jams, we wallow in a corrosive bath of hormones. Even though it's not life or death, we hyperventilate, our hearts pound, muscles tense. Ironically, after a while, the stress response is more damaging than the stressor itself because the stressor is some

psychological nonsense that you're falling for..."

Athletic Translation: "We turn on the exact same stress response thinking about how we messed up so badly and how we let everyone down. Toxic thoughts about losing our position, choking under pressure, the last failure pops up over and over again and the key difference is we're not doing it for any real good reason. It's just our chatter "chasing-cats" and we're doing it non-stop.

What a classic line, "psychological nonsense that we fall for". The psychological nonsense is all that negative, toxic chatter that's going on in your head throughout the day. By allowing the chatter to run rampant, the chatter becomes our own worst enemy from within. You must learn how to recognize the enemy so you can deal harshly even when you find it within yourself.

11.1 Movie Scene: Peaceful Warrior

Recently, I had the privilege of sitting with Emanuel "Manny" Arceneaux. If you follow Manny, he graduated from a small town in Louisiana and worked hard to earn the chance to play college and professional football in the National and Canadian Football Leagues. Manny and his experiences represent a wonderful story of never giving up in the chatter and beating the odds.

During one of his return trips home we had the chance to meet and talk what I call the "seventh level". Deep intimate conversation about how he deals with the chatter and all the disruptive emotions.

Manny said to me, Peaceful Warrior. It's a movie that every athlete needs to watch. Manny went on say that he watches this movie every night before a big game. A classic for your personal library, it is based on the true story of Olympian Dan Millman. Millman represented the United States in 1966 winning four gold metals in gymnastics.

Millman's book, Way of the Peaceful Warrior was brought to the big screen in 2006. In the movie, Nick Nolte (nicknamed "Socrates") is coaching Millman who at the time is a young aspiring Olympian athlete.

The coaching, however, is on the mental game. The entire movie is about Millman's struggle with the mental game and learning to regulate the chatter.

Throughout the movie it is clear Millman has a strong work ethic. He applies the daily physical training with hours upon end repeating the routines and exercises. Millman, like most athletes, focus intensely and entirely on the physical regimen. The entire movie is about his struggle with the idea that athletic performance is as much mental as it is physical.

There are many scenes that drive home and illustrate these complicated truths about how your chatter affects performance. In one scene, Socrates says to the young athlete, "Take out the trash". Millman's character smarts off, "You take out the trash; it's your trash!" Socrates replies, "No, no, the trash in your head. Over half what goes on up there is trash...you need to learn how to take out the trash in your head."

This is your same action item in learning these mental skills. Learn to get the negative chatter out of your head, all words and mental pictures that stand in your way of optimal performance. When you let the chatter run with no awareness, no regulation, it's just negative crap that creates what science calls "frazzle" and the classic fight, flight or freeze is your best prediction on how you will perform when the pressure is on.

You have an intelligent brain. It's a very complicated thing. No other creature on God's green earth has it designed exactly like only you. As a human being, you have this amazing ability to learn, listen and change your thoughts.

11.2.1 Guiding Principle: Imagination Rules

In your imagination you never lose; the picture is always perfect, the task execution is always excellent. In your imagination, each domino from your task falls into place with ease and execution as if to say to yourself, "Well done good and faithful warrior".

The beautiful thing about the imagination is that your mind does not know the difference between the chatter and reality. The pictures you see with your eyes and the mental pictures that appear in thought are handled in a very similar way.

This lesson can be difficult to teach but you must seek to understand that your chatter and your reality are basically processed the same way inside your brain. When you learn the proper steps to visualization techniques you are pre-programming the mind for each task, every emotion and the words and mental pictures to support you, in advance. For now, accept this idea as we continue to move forward understanding the power of your chatter when it comes to regulating for the future.

You are going to daydream and imagine at times. It's what we do. It's the way you are built. What we are striving for in our development is to daydream and refine these ideas that mean much to you. When you daydream enough and some images repeat often you turn these hazy dreams into goals for the future. By using mental skills you then re-enforce with purpose and reason, this is what we teach as emotional intensity.

As you sit here now today in a new level of

awareness to the 86,400 seconds of your day, there are specific things you should be thinking, specific words and mental pictures given your goals and your ambitions. The things you want to achieve you must now develop mental and emotional skills and flex your chatter on demand to support you. If you're looking forward and thinking about your next practice, your next chance the coach is going to look at you, then there is specific chatter you should be disciplining inside.

If you want to be two hundred and thirty pounds with twelve percent body fat there are specific physical-disciplines that you must do every day, throughout the day. Based on the new definition of strong there are specific mental-disciplines that you must do every day, throughout the day and it all starts with your chatter.

11.2.2 Guiding Principle: Vivid Images

When you imagine and truly exercise your ability to visualize yourself taking action you must be clear and detailed in your mental pictures. Your mind will not work well with general thoughts and casual words and casual mental pictures. You must be very clear and very specific with your inner dialogue. You must go behind the casual and drill down into your own personal "seventh-level" reasons and define specifically what mental pictures you want and your own personal motives for wanting them.

You can't just say, "Well, I'm going to make that block. I'm going make that throw or I am going to do better." The brain doesn't do well with general words like this. You can't just tell the missile, "Just go over there and take out that target." You have to be very specific with detailed "x" and "y" coordinates to achieve the objective. And then, as the missile takes off, it has an on-board navigation to adapt and make changes to ensure an accurate strike. You have this same ability. In your 86,400 seconds of this day, when you are specific in regulating your chatter, you can navigate disruptive thoughts and emotions on demand ensuring wise decision-making for the greater good.

You are focused and flexing your mental skills; meaning you're feeding the chatter the words and the mental pictures day-in and day-out, knowing you're going to stray, knowing you're going to get negative. You are now going to grab the chatter, regulate it and no longer struggle with the idea or the self-discipline required.

11.2.3 Guiding Principle: Filters

There was an old America On Line (AOL) commercial a few years back that really summoned it all up nicely,

"Life needs filters; chatter needs filters"

Your brain needs a filter 86,400 seconds of each day or your chatter will run wild. That's why these are called mental skills; they require effort and work on your behalf to filter out the trashy-talk.

The key is recovery, using your mental skills to recover from negative chatter and an emotional highjack. This is not about preventing negative chatter. It's not about stopping the negative feelings or having negative thoughts. It's about your skill and your ability to recover from a negative thought. I've been practicing these ideas for over thirty years and I still get high jacked. It's my ability at that moment to catch the chatter and discipline it, in order to recover.

11.3 Exercise: Reflection #2

We tried this exercise earlier; it's one you should practice often. Reflect back with purpose, reason and discipline, rather than reflecting back with damaging mental pictures.

Shut your eyes and rewind the game film in your mind. Think back using words and mental pictures. Pull up scenes and emotions during a moment when you made the play and surprised yourself, it was clearly a time when you were at peak optimal performance. Stop for a minute. Think back.

Everyday you must learn to celebrate your achievements by reflecting back. These are the subtle "penny" moments that nourish the path for today and tomorrow promising bigger, better and brighter moments.

Your greatest achievements are worthy of reflecting. A skilled, disciplined chatter to reflect and review each domino you performed when executing the task.

"Reflection is the school of wisdom; requiring a disciplined chatter"

11.4.1 Guiding Principle: Personal Agenda

This is personal, after all these mental skills and the promise of the future belong to you. All of what we talk about in this book references what goes on inside of you. Only you know, only you can be responsible and only you can hold yourself accountable to these ideas and development strategies.

"Your imagination is your own limitation."

If you can conceive it and think it into your chatter, then you can believe it in your emotions, creating an opportunity to achieve it.

Don't let anyone steal your chatter or your dreams. As soon as it comes in, your awareness and regulation skills "take-out-the-trash" on demand. It's your gig. Right here. Regulating the chatter. Flexing your mental muscle. You can do this.

"I see myself beyond my current circumstances with new words and mental pictures"

There are times you must use these words in your chatter. You will physically practice a task thousands and thousands of hours, over and over and over again. You have trained your body and your physical domain. Now you must train the mental and emotional domains. Your true health condition is now redefined as physical, mental and emotional. You must monitor all three on a regular basis.

At the end of the day, here are specific "x" and "y" coordinates for you to communicate, concentrate, organize, discriminate, and innovate. Hold yourself-accountable.

At the end of the day, let the chatter dominate these words and core values…

- *"I am competing against my own last performance."*

- *"Everyone else competing is only there to keep me honest."*

- *"Others define the level of play; I must achieve these results and redefine."*

- *"When I achieve these results, I earn the opportunity to compete."*

Notes & Quotes:

1. Dr. Daniel Goleman - Latest findings on the brain: Emotional Intelligence Webinar

   - www.danielgoleman.info

2. Robert Sapolsky – Stanford University Professor, "Distress: The Body's Silent Killer" – National Geographic Documentary

   - http://www.thegreatcourses.com/tgc/professors/professor_detail.aspx?pid=124

3. History Channel's Documentary: "The Brain" 2013

4. Les Brown – Author, public speaker

   - http://lesbrown.com/

5. Jim Rohn – Author, public speaker

   - http://www.jimrohn.com/

6. Dr. Jeff Garrison – Sport Medicine, Former NFL player

Special thanks:

To my dear friend, Molly Daniels, thank you so much for taking the time to edit and put your writing skills and expertise to good work. It is because of you these ideas are refined and the quality of this message has been improved.

- http://mollydaniels.wordpress.com/

To all those who have encouraged, remained patient and persevered on my behalf by continuing to stay on me. As God as my witness, your words remained in my chatter and were a critical part of making this dream become a reality.

Be sure to visit online at www.ParrishTaylor.com. Our website is designed as a support tool with regular updates to assist you in personal growth. To learn more about live learning events or custom development plans, please visit on line of or by calling 866-487-2815.

Made in the USA
Monee, IL
13 January 2022